PAX INTRANTIBUS

BOOKS BY FREDERICK SMOCK

POETRY
Gardencourt
The Good Life
Guest House
Sonnets

PROSE
This Meadow of Time: A Provence Journal
Poetry & Compassion: Essays on Art & Craft

EDITOR
The American Voice Anthology of Poetry

PAX INTRANTIBUS

*A Meditation on the Poetry
of Thomas Merton*

Frederick Smock

BROADSTONE BOOKS

An embryonic version of this monograph appeared in *The Merton Seasonal,* Vol. 27 (Bellarmine College), and in *Poetry & Compassion: Essays on Art & Craft* (Wind Publications). The author is grateful to these editors, to Jonathan Montaldo and Dr. Paul Pearson, and to his wife Olga-Maria Cruz for their guidance and support.

LIBRARY OF CONGRESS CONTROL NUMBER: 2006932462

ISBN-10: 0-9721144-6-7
ISBN-13: 978-0-9721144-6-2

COPYRIGHT © 2007 BY FREDERICK SMOCK

BROADSTONE BOOKS
AN IMPRINT OF BROADSTONE MEDIA LLC
418 ANN STREET
FRANKFORT, KY 40601-1929
BroadstoneBooks.com

to Olga-Maria

&

to my sons, Sam and Ben

ACKNOWLEDGMENTS

Quotations from the poetry of Thomas Merton is used by permission as follows: "Untitled Poem" by Thomas Merton from *Eighteen Poems,* Copyright © 1949 by Our Lady of Gethsemani Abbey; "Song for Our Lady of Cobre," "The Flight into Egypt," and "The Trappist Abbey: Matins," Copyright © 1944 by Our Lady of Gethsemani Monastery; "City after Noon," "The Ohio River—Louisville," Copyright © 1946 by New Directions Publishing Corp.;"For My Brother: Reported Missing in Action, 1943;" "The Night of Destiny," "The Peril," Copyright © 1948 by New Directions Publishing Corp.; "Elegy for the Monastery Barn," "In Silence," "The Guns of Fort Knox," "Wisdom," Copyright © 1957 by The Abbey of Gethsemani; "Original Child Bomb," Copyright © 1962 by The Abbey of Gethsemani; "A Letter to Pablo Antonio Cuadra Concerning Giants," "Chant to Be Used in Processions Around a Site with Furnaces," "Man is Born in Tao," Copyright © 1963 by The Abbey of Gethsemani; "The Man of Tao," Copyright © 1965 by The Abbey of Gethsemani; "Cables to the Ace," Copyright © 1968 by The Abbey of Gethsemani; "A Clever Stratagem or, How to Handle Mystics," "The Geography of Lograire: Ten Guns Are Out of Work Up Anger Hollow," Copyright © 1968, 1969 by The Trustees of the Merton Legacy Trust; and "Readings from Ibn Abbad," Copyright © 1977 by The Trustees of the Merton Legacy Trust; reprinted from *The Collected Poems of Thomas Merton* by permission of New Directions Publishing Corp.

PAX INTRANTIBUS

Did I fulfill what I had to, here, on earth?
I was a guest in a house under white clouds
Where rivers flow and grasses renew themselves.
So what if I were called, if I was hardly aware.
The next time early I would search for wisdom.

—Czeslaw Milosz,
from *One More Contradiction*

PREFACE

You, *the reader, perhaps need no preface. Except for me to say that this meditation on the Trappist monk Thomas Merton's poetry takes the shape of an extended inquiry into his methods and ideas, chiefly, his ideas about peace. Peace-work gave shape to much of his poetry—a secular liturgy of the will. This book also considers poetry as an act of political engagement—Merton models for us what many poets and artists do, that is, dream of a better world.*

"All generalities are dangerous, even this one," Alexander Dumas observed. Nobody—especially not Merton—can be contained in a phrase, or a book. When I speak of Merton, what do I know for certain? Father Matthew Kelty, one of Merton's colleagues at the Abbey of Gethsemani, once said to a student of mine, "It would be as difficult to bottle Merton as it would be to bottle fog."

There have been many studies published about Merton's life and work, but relatively few about his poetry. Merton shares a great deal with the ancient Chinese poet-monks, and, in their fashion, I have been tempted to write lengthy chapter titles, such as, "Sitting on Cold Mountain During a Spring Rain-shower and Hearing the Monastery Call to Prayers, I Think About Merton's Imagery of the Bell." In the end, I let the prose stand alone. Associative as it is. Intuitive as it is. One poet to another. In peace.

~ F.S.

I.

The night artillery range at Fort Knox was one of the familiar sounds of my childhood. At the time, however, I did not know what those soft plosive thuds might be. Fort Knox lay some fifty miles southwest of Louisville, distance enough to muffle the explosions of shells. Lying on my narrow bed at night, with my window propped open to the sounds of traffic on Barret Avenue, and the bells of St.-Therése tolling the quarter-hours, occasional sirens and dogs barking in the neighboring blocks—through it all, underneath it all, stole the soft thuddings of a distant something that I barely registered, and certainly could not identify. These explosions dropped in among the other sounds of the city night, small as commas, punctuating the darkness. Some nights I could not hear them at all. The winds had shifted, or I was not paying attention; I was thinking of other things, intent upon images from my day, or intent upon dreams. I could not hear the sounds unless (it seems to me now) I had assumed the silent and alert attitude of prayer.

At the abbey of Gethsemani, thirty-five miles south of Louisville, the Trappist monk Thomas Merton lay on his narrow bed listening to these same bursting noises, his sleep troubled. He knew full well what they were. He wrote about them in his poem "The Guns of Fort Knox:"

> Guns at the camp (I hear them suddenly)
> Guns make the little houses jump. I feel
> Explosions in my feet, through boards.
> Wars work under the floor. Wars
> Dance in the foundations. Trees
> Must also feel the guns they do not want
> Even in their core.
> As each charge bumps the shocked earth
> They shudder from the root.

The subterranean, almost hellish aspect of these exploding artillery shells is no mere conceit in this poem. Those sounds actually came up through the floorboards – I felt them as much as heard them, coming up from under my bed – and not through the air, as one might have expected. They were strong enough to wake the dead. But that, Merton wrote, would not be the right resurrection. "Let them sleep on, / O guns," he wrote, thinking not only of the dead but also, perhaps, of the living – the sleeping children, like me.

Not until a few years later, when I read the above poem of Merton's, did I understand what those sounds were. Merton named them for me – they were military ordnance exploding. I began to understand, then, the power of poetry to give a name to the nameless. All wisdom is rooted in learning to call things by their right names, Confucius said. That was just practice shelling we heard, of course, Merton and I. Dummy shells. Many children around the world go to sleep with the sound of real shells exploding, ringing in their ears. They go to sleep, or do not go to sleep, knowing that the guns are aimed at them, and that the shells are real. I was lucky. But the shells that I heard, that Merton heard, remain an allegory of the real violence that exists in so much of the world.

II.

M<small>Y GRANDMOTHER</small> lived on a cul-de-sac off Barrett Avenue, in Louisville, next to the Altenheim, an old-folks home founded by German nuns. I lived with my grandmother when I was a child. From our house, we often walked down to Broadway and caught the street-car to 4th Street, the center of town, lively with stores and restaurants, movie-houses and jazz clubs. We walked up 4th Street to Walnut Street, an intersection famous for Stewart's department store, the Seelbach Hotel (mentioned in *The Great Gatsby*) and the venerable men's shops of the Starks building. This was the very heart of the city. And it was here, on a Tuesday, March 19, 1958, that Merton experienced his famous revelation. As he wrote in his journal for that day:

> In the center of the shopping district, I was suddenly overwhelmed with the realization that I loved all these people, that they were mine and I was theirs, that we could not be alien to one another even though we were total strangers.... I have the immense joy of being human, a member of the race in which God himself became incarnate. As if the sorrows and stupidities of the human condition could overwhelm me, now that I realize what we all are. If only everybody could realize this! But it cannot be explained. There is no way of telling people that they are all walking around shining like the sun.

Do I like to imagine that I was there that day, holding on to my grandmother's hand, both of us walking around shining like the sun? Yes, I do. I would have been almost five years old. We would have been going about our errands in the shops up and down 4th Street, before catching the street-car back home. Who would not have wanted to be one of Merton's beautiful people? To have been a part of that glorious moment—in which a small man with a beatific face (the face of "the only hillbilly who knows where the still is," he said of himself) experienced a moment of divine bliss, and conferred upon all of us a blessing of the purest origin.

Merton's ecstatic moment—a famous one among Merton scholars—is referred to in the literature as either an *epiphany* or a *revelation*. There does seem to me a fine distinction between these two modes of knowing. An epiphany comes from within; a revelation comes from without. Merton's word for it, realization, does not help us to choose.

III.

ONE OF THE SHOPS along 4th Street was W. K. Stewart's, a bookstore of high mahogany shelves and well-oiled clerks, all older men who seemed inwardly possessed of the secrets that, I felt certain, those many books held. Those sleek men intimidated me. My first few visits to the store—after I had learned to read, and when I had a little spending money of my own—I conducted clandestinely. I slipped into the store, looked about surreptitiously for a while, then slipped out again. I did not dare ask the clerks for help. What was I looking for, anyway? I scanned the books on their shelves as if looking for a familiar face in the crowd, lost and alone.

One of those days, I actually took a couple of books down off a shelf of poetry. These would be the first books I bought. I was maybe twelve years old. One of them was Yevgeny Yevtushenko's *Stolen Apples*. I remember turning to the title poem, and reading its concluding lament, "To whom does God pray / when He tires of our entreaties?" Even as a boy, I felt profoundly moved. The lines still move me. (A few years ago, I gave a reading of my own poems at a Russian émigré center in New York City, and, when asked, acknowledged that Yevtushenko had been one of my earliest influences. There came a grumbling from the small audience—Yevtushenko has the reputation of a Soviet apologist. Nonetheless, I defended my naïve choice on purely poetical grounds.)

The other book I pulled off that same shelf that day and took home with me was Merton's *Selected Poems*, which had come out in 1959. Merton knew well my hometown of Louisville, and he wrote of things that I knew about—the muddy Ohio River, for example:

> No one can hear the loud voice of the city
> Because of the tremendous silence
> Of this slow-moving river, quiet as space.
>
> Not the towering bridge, the crawling train,
> Nor the knives of pylons
> Clashing in the sun....
>
>   "The Ohio River, Louisville"

My grandmother and I sometimes took the 4th Street car all the way down to the Second Street bridge, near where her husband (long dead) had owned a drugstore. We leaned on the railing at the River Road turnaround and looked out at the deep-moving river, the most noble river in the world, in historian H. H. McMurtrie's phrase. Merton helped to focus my young eyes, and the river moved me in new ways.

Mostly, though, I have to say that I do not know why I chose Merton's book. Years later, when working in a bookstore during graduate school, I learned that people buy books for sometimes mysterious reasons. The book "speaks" to them, or simply feels right in the hand. A line or two cursorily read might hold a glimmer of a better life, or an answer sought. Something intuitive is at work here. The book is saying, *Perhaps not now but someday you will need to read me.*

So, my first and abiding sense of Merton is as a poet. Somewhere within myself, I became aware of the devotional aspect of his poems, though I do not think I named this to myself at the time. But he spoke of wonder and mystery and joy, and, certainly, this had been my experience of the world up till then. I lived with my grandmother and mother and great-aunt in a big house in the city—a whole community of women. They doted on me and I returned their affection. (It was a kind of pediatric harem.) Widows next door, and a whole house of nuns at the end of the cul-de-sac, also pampered me, the only young male on the court—World War II was only a decade past. And so, when Merton spoke of the power and beauty of creation, I felt that I knew what he meant when he wrote:

> Hearing with what joy this child of God
> Plays in the perfect garden of her martyrdom....
> Spending the silver of her little life
> To bring her Bridegroom these bright flowers
> Of which her arms are full....
> Her virtues, with their simple strings,
> Play to the Lover hidden in the universe.

IV.

M‍ERTON CAME TO believe that Kentucky occupies the center of the universe. He journeyed to Kentucky from his natal France via Cambridge and New York. His decision to become a Trappist, on the eve of America's entry into World War II, came in "an instant," he said. While reading the *Catholic Encyclopedia* entry on Carthusian monks, suddenly "the desire of those solitudes was wide open within me like a wound."

On St. Lucy's Day, December 13, he was accepted as a postulant and moved into the monastery. "Gethsemani," he wrote, "is more beautiful than any place I ever went to for its beauty." For a while, he participated in the full life of the abbey. Soon after his ordination to the priesthood, in 1949, Merton was appointed director of scholastics, responsible for the formation of monks. Later, he became director of novices. He satisfied his craving for solitude with long walks in the woods, and with stolen hours writing in a shed he nicknamed St. Anne's.

He lived in the abbey for twenty-four years. Then he retreated, into the piney woods, to his hermitage, a concrete-block cabin he called St. Mary of Carmel, where he received permission in 1965 from the Vatican to live full-time. In retreat, he believed, "One can live at a good, quiet, productive tempo–manual labor in the morning, writing in the afternoon," he wrote in his journal for August 25 of that year, the feast of St. Louis, his namesake. (The reader will not find Merton buried under his birth name at the abbey; his marker, a small white cross like all the others in the monks' graveyard, reports only his monastic name, Father Louis.)

He wrote and published prolifically, on theology, on literature and world religions, and also in protest of the war in Vietnam and against nuclear proliferation, capitalist excess and industrial blight. He communicated with such varied figures as the Dalai Lama, Boris Pasternak, Joan Baez, and Czeslaw Milosz. "His intellectual life was as thoroughly engaged as that of any of his secular contemporaries," writes John Jeremiah Sullivan, in the *Oxford American*. "That he should have been a monk, and a hermit for many years at that, is really a lovely irony: a broad, roving mind confronting the world, and a soul at rest in a Kentucky cabin."

"I walk in the woods out of necessity," Merton wrote, in his journal of May, 1965. "I am both a prisoner and an escaped prisoner. I cannot tell you why, born in France, my journey ended here in Kentucky. I have considered going further, but it is not practical." When he first arrived at Gethsemani, and walked under the gate bearing the inscription, P*ax Intrantibus* –Peace Those who Enter–he wrote in his journal, "This is the center of America. I had wondered what was holding the country together, what has been keeping the universe from cracking in pieces and falling apart. It is this monastery...."

Gethsemani lies east of Bardstown, Kentucky, where the cattle farmers paint "Beef–it's what's for dinner" on their barns, where one is likely to get stuck behind a back-hoe on the main road, and where, earlier in the century, my father's family owned the Talbott Tavern, a local watering hole. The tavern dates to the 18th century, when it was a stage-coach stop. Merton often stopped in for a beer with James Laughlin, his publisher, or with fellow poet Jonathan Greene, and jazz musicians like Richard Sisto (Merton played bongos), among many others.

Laughlin has written about how he would collect

Merton at the monastery in his black motorcar. Merton would come running out in his robes with a bundle under his arm. Around the first bend, they stopped, Merton ran into the woods and changed into overalls, then they continued on to Louisville, for an afternoon of gallery hopping and beer-drinking. Coming home, Merton would run into the woods at the bend in the road and change back into his robes.

The land spreading around the abbey, he declared, is "the most beautiful place in America. I never saw anything like the country. A very wide valley—full of rolling and dipping land, woods, cedars, dark green fields—maybe young wheat.... And in the window comes the good smell of full fields—*agri pleni.*"

An historical note: The first Cistercian abbey had been established in 1098 in the wilderness of France, and a grandson abbey in 1142 near Nantes, called Melleray. It was from Melleray, some seven hundred years later, that a party of monks set out for the wilderness of Nelson County, Kentucky. Their aim was the same as those first Cistercians—union with God, peace, and simplicity.

V.

A MONASTERY IS a place apart from the known world, where, in Merton's words, one can "entertain silence in the heart and listen for the voice of God–to pray for your own discovery."

Hospitality has always been at the core of the mission of monasteries. According to St. Benedict's *Rule for Monasteries,* the guest represents Christ, no less, and has a claim on the welcome of the monastic community. Gethsemani has been taking in guests since its founding in 1848. The only thing they ask of guests is: silence. "Communing with the Lord requires a measure of solitude, a stillness and an emptiness, a waiting on and attending to the Spirit," reads the Gethsemani brochure. "Silence fosters and preserves the climate of prayer and is thus a fundamental part of the retreat experience."

A monastery opens its doors to applicants, who are always strangers at first knocking, as well as to those wishing to be guests only for a while. Both kinds of strangers arrive in order to retreat from the world, and, whatever their reasons, the monastery doors stand open.

Merton retreated further and further from the

known world—first to the abbey, then to his hermitage, and then, when the hermitage became too accessible to guests, he traveled to California, New Mexico, and Alaska looking for possible new sites for a hermitage. Of course, Merton enjoyed and even encouraged those many guests who visited him at Gethsemani. At the same time, he keenly felt the limitations they imposed upon him. He had little enough time to write and pray already, given his duties at the abbey. And yet, given his steady stream of visitors, he proved to be terrifically prolific. He is prolific even into the posthumous phase of his career.

Merton's search for a pure retreat, where, in his words, "you cast your care upon the Lord," led him eventually to the Far East. Had he not died unexpectedly in Bangkok, would he have returned to Kentucky? Might he have found a sanctuary in, say, Kyoto, the ancient city of temples? Or Alaska? He wrote in a 1968 letter to Fr. Flavian Burns, his abbot, "My feeling at present is that Alaska is certainly the ideal place for solitude and the hermit life." Might he have found there the solitude and the solace that seemed to have escaped him everywhere else?

As he wrote in "The City After Noon":

What if the wild contentment were full
And there were nothing left in the world
But fields, water and sun
And space went on forever to eternity, without a river?

His travels had already taken him from France to England to America. Now, he sought an openness beyond all borders. Was he looking for something not to be found on this earth?

VI.

A FEW YEARS AGO, I visited Merton's hermitage in the woods. On a rainy Saturday in March, when the dogwoods had just blossomed—snowy white petals against gray skies—I fell in with a small band of retreatants at the abbey, and one of the brothers led us back a cart-path through the piney woods to Merton's cinder-block cabin. The hermitage is perhaps a familiar image—it has been much photographed—the squared-off cabin among slender white trees, low-slung porch, woodpile off to one side. To step inside the cabin is to enjoy a rare point of view, like stepping into a photograph and looking out. That day, perhaps because it was raining, it felt like stepping behind a waterfall—an enraptured place where, when the skies clear, the rainbow ends, or begins.

We built a fire in the hearth. We prayed, read

poems, talked in hushed tones. Some of us made notes in small moleskin journals. We gazed out the windows at the rain rinsing clean the day. We sat in silent meditation. "Silence has many dimensions," Merton wrote, in *Creative Silence*. "It can be a regression and an escape, a loss of self, or it can be presence, awareness, unification, self-awareness." Referencing Paul Tillich's phrase, "the courage to be," Merton continued, "Positive silence pulls us together and makes us realize who we are, who we might be, and the distance between those two."

"What do I really want to do?" Merton had asked himself, in his journal of June 21, 1959. And he answered himself, "Long hours of quiet in the woods, reading a little, meditating a lot, walking up and down in the pine needles in bare feet."

His hermitage (a closely protected place, by the way) looked much the same as Merton left it, we were told. The back room held a narrow bed and a small stack of books, with three cassocks hanging in an alcove. The kitchen, which is only a wide place in the hall, held a sink, hot-plate, small refrigerator, and the only framed item in the place—a certificate from the Vatican conferring upon him the designation "Hermit." His front room held the writing table, bookcase, rocking chair, and those large unadorned windows with a generous view of the woods and the cart-path meandering into the distance.

The only decoration remains a cross, in bas-relief,

in the limestone over the fireplace, now blackened around the edges by years of wood-smoke. It seemed a sign. "What struggles the man must have endured within these walls," one of us said aloud. Not a man of a serene faith, Merton struggled over the years to reconcile his earthly nature with his divine calling. "You cannot be a man of faith," he says to us, in *New Seeds of Contemplation,* "unless you know how to doubt."

Doubt is never allayed by officiousness, severity, or correctness, though these things might look like solutions. "I know, Sister, that solitude / Will never dismay you," he wrote, in the poem "To a Severe Nun."

Meditating at his hearth, browsing his bookshelves, we found ourselves in imaginary society with Merton. The quality of our contemplation might have been relatively poor. Still, we were breathing the same air, and walking barefoot up and down in the same pine needles. We also read a number of his poems that speak to the notion of retreat itself. I remember with particular clarity a stanza from his poem "In Silence":

> Who (be quiet)
> Are you (as these stones
> Are quiet). Do not
> Think of what you are
> Still less of
> What you may one day be.
> Rather

> Be what you are (but who?) be
> The unthinkable one
> You do not know.

The secular writer shares a great deal with a poet-monk—the desire for solitude, the sanctity of work, the desire for some kind of transcendental affirmation, and the discovery of the self. And yet, lest we take ourselves too seriously, Merton wrote in his journal for January 15, 1963, "The best thing about the retreat has been working in the pig barn...."

When the woods began to grow dark, near time for vespers, we closed up the cabin and trekked back. We were not quite the same people who had come out that noon, nor was it quite the same world to which we returned. We were more capacious. "Art pushes out the boundaries of our universe a little bit," Salman Rushdie said to me in conversation one day. And that is something of what we felt—that our boundaries had been pushed out a little bit. And if the change within us was incomplete, at least our new capacity had prepared us for it.

VII.

The casual visitor to Merton's hermitage can come away, after even a brief spell, with a feeling of serenity. But Merton was not about serenity, even if he might have wished it so. His search for peace – personal, political, spiritual – pushed him to the ends of the earth, eventually leading him halfway around the world. His interior life careened between restlessness and paradox: He was a voluble man who observed monastic silence. He was a lover of women who took a vow of chastity. He was a best-selling author who renounced worldly goods. And yet, he clearly found inspiring – and inspiriting – the limitations imposed upon him as a member of a strict monastic order.

Merton came to believe that a monk in the 20th century cannot wall himself off from the world. The Vatican tried to silence him. He tried to silence himself. But he could not be silent. Despite his hermit ways (or because of them?), Merton became a prominent voice of dissent in this power-mad nation. He became, almost against his will, a monk of social and political engagement. He openly deplored the mentality of the Cold War – the Russians do not need to build so many bombs, Merton declared, we Americans are busy destroying ourselves – and he firmly criticized the undeclared U.S. war in Vietnam. (Numerous South Vietnamese Buddhist monks chose to protest that war by self-immolation.) Like the Desert Fathers, those 4th-century Christian ascetics, Merton felt he had the duty to pull the world to safety. And he expressed that duty most clearly in his poetry.

Sometimes, he confessed, he felt like opting out of the peace movement. "I am rather tired of being a human," he wrote in a 1962 letter to James Roy Newman, "and would enjoy being a nice quiet civilized fish, without political affiliations." A fish, I imagine, floating in the eternal element of its own being, immersed in mystery. A fish that would not be civilized by our standards, but by its own. A fish, perhaps, like the one in Merton's translation of this poem by Chuang Tzu, a 3rd-century Chinese Taoist—

> Fishes are born in water.
> Man is born in Tao.
> If fishes, born in water,
> Seek the deep shadow
> Of pond and pool,
> All their needs
> Are satisfied.
> If man, born in Tao,
> Sinks into the deep shadow
> Of non-action
> To forget aggression and concern,
> He lacks nothing,
> His life is secure.

Merton became a poet-monk very much in the tradition of Tu Fu, Wang Wei, and Han Shan before him. Like them, his poems are signs left to mark the way he traveled, notches on his walking stick. The greatest among the wandering poet-monks was Bashō, whose *Narrow Road to the Deep North* detailed his wanderings, punctuated by haiku, which marked the trail—

> A wanderer,
> let that be my name—
> the first winter rain

Over the centuries, Arabian kings of antiquity, elderly Asian poets, and other manner of old men have taken to the highway in their dotage, to die amid the world's bounty, to meet eternity half-way. In middle age, Merton took to the road that led eastward, though he could not have known how close to death he was.

VIII.

MERTON CAME to his God through poetry. At Columbia, he studied William Blake. "As Blake worked himself into my system," Merton writes in *Seven Storey*

Mountain, "I became more and more conscious of the necessity of a vital faith, and of the total unreality and unsubstantiality of the dead, selfish rationalism which had been freezing my mind and will…. I became conscious of the fact that the only way to live was to live in a world that was charged with the presence and reality of God."

Blake had seen the prophet Elijah standing beside a tree in the south of London. Blake spoke to angels, and they spoke to him. Blake believed that the Catholic Church alone taught the love of God. He wrote, "The Religions of all Nations are derived from each Nation's different reception of the Poetic Genius [that is, capacity for imaginative vision], which is everywhere call'd the Spirit of Prophecy." Merton perhaps found an inspiration for his humanistic ecumenism in such lines as these, from Blake's "The Divine Image:"

> …all must love the human form,
> In heathen, Turk, or Jew.
> Where Mercy, Love, & Pity dwell,
> There God is dwelling too.

Blake wrote these words in a place and time – 18th-century England – when Turks and Jews were the objects of particular scorn. Here, Blake proves himself a visionary, and an artist of an advanced sensitivity. I think Merton is in harmony with Blake, especially when he writes, in *New Seeds of Contemplation,* "A Catholic poet should be an apostle by being first of all a poet, not try to be a poet by being first of all an apostle." The vision Blake extended to Merton led him toward a mystical spirituality, one highly charged by the Word. Merton came to write his master's thesis at Columbia on Blake, by which time, he acknowledged, "the groundwork of conversion was more or less complete."

Merton's conversion (from paganism, he claimed) came on the eve of World War II, after his experience in Cuba. At the church of St. Francis in Havana, he sat listening to a children's choir singing in pure round notes, *Yo creo, yo creo* ("I believe, I believe"). As he wrote in his journal, he suddenly felt overwhelmed with "the unshakeable certainty, the clear and immediate knowledge that heaven was right in front of me."

One day he traveled out to Our Lady of Cobre, where, in 1687, the Virgin Mary was said to have appeared to three slave girls. He found the basilica empty, save for an old lady dressed all in black, who would not leave him to pray alone in peace. Thus spied upon, Merton knelt before La Caridad, the black Virgin, and tried to make his prayers. He returned, somewhat disappointed, to Santiago. But there, sitting on the terrace of his hotel, La Caridad handed him a poem. Written in a kind of rapture, "Song for Our Lady of Cobre," Merton would later say, became the first real poem he had ever written:

> The white girls lift their heads like trees,
> The black girls go
> Reflected like flamingoes in the street.
>
> The white girls sing as shrill as water,
> The black girls talk as quiet as clay...

For Merton, as for W. H. Auden,* poetry and spirituality became inextricably linked. Merton had not been able to write real poems, he would say later, until becoming a Catholic.

When he returned from Cuba to New York City, Merton would lie on his bed and flip indolently through the *Spiritual Exercises* of St. Ignatius, casting it aside repeatedly to look more excitedly through his travel brochures of Mexico, Cuba, Brazil.

Merton's experience of the Word—in the pure lyrical voices of children, in the ethereal whisper of La Caridad—led him straight to his God. What peace he found there, in the humblest of circumstances, became a peace that he would try to extend, through prayers and poems, to a war-crazed world. Working for peace gave a definite shape to Merton's spiritual life. And, in his poetry, he achieved a kind of literary grace, balancing his artistic and devotional sensibilities.

---

*Auden had rebutted a schoolmate's attack on the Catholic Church by claiming to be a believer, then, to make peace, asked his friend if he wrote poetry. Auden later recollected this event in "Letter to Lord Byron": *Kicking a little stone, he turned to me / And said, "Tell me, do you write poetry?" / I never had, and said so, but I knew / That very moment what I wished to do.*

As Blake sought to call down an ecstatic vision to this earth (and, indeed, he did see visions), Merton followed a path of poetic revelation, culminating in *Cables to the Ace,* which he subtitled *Familiar Liturgies of Misunderstanding.* His last fully realized collection, *Cables* pushes for an absolute freedom of mentality and spirituality. (Merton claimed that *Cables* could be read forward or backward with similar results.) The poet-monk exults in a language at once fantastic and tragic. Section 36:

> Eve moves: golden Mother of baroque lights. She visits a natural supermarket of naked fruits. She wings her perfumes. Le poil humide de ses aisselles. T.S. Eliot is vexed and cannot look.

The reference to Eliot is telling. Merton has announced, This is not your father's poem. This is not your father's faith.

Cables, actually, is a kind of antipoetry, "a sequence of *non sequiturs,*" Merton wrote in a working notebook, "an underground logic of association in conflict with the apparent demands of logical communication." Poet Lynn Szabo comments that, in *Cables,* "his poetic voice synthesizes the forces of his multifaceted consciousness—ranging from the quiet romanticism and piety of the earlier poems to the eclecticism of *Emblems of a Season of Fury*... which had integrated his longtime concern with social unrest and his experience with Zen." If this poem is noisy, crude, and imprecise, as Merton described it in a letter to Cid Corman, then it is also free of the constraints and degradations of language that Merton saw in the general culture, and this freedom makes possible a great beauty and lyricism, transcendence even:

> Slowly slowly
> Comes Christ through the garden
> Speaking to the sacred trees
> Their branches bear his light without harm

IX.

ALL OF THE GREAT THINKERS of our age have been brought round to the question: How are we to prevent war?

Einstein wondered how "little we are justified in leaving the struggle against armaments and against the war spirit to governments... the best method in this case is the violent one—conscientious objection, [to make] the problem of pacifism an acute one, a real struggle to which forceful spirits will be attracted." For him, this was an absolute position.

Virginia Woolf, in her book *Three Guineas,* makes

the argument (though she admits it might be doomed) that education offers the best hope. Woolf's single teaching experience was not a positive one, however. She found herself staring across a gulf of wealth and privilege at a classroom filled with factory girls to whom she had surprisingly little to say.

Pope John XXIII, in his Christmas address of 1961, urged the world's leaders to shun all thought of force. But is this possible for the martial masculine mind?

Merton decided that the cause of all wars is sin. Because, he said, we all bear a responsibility for the world, through grace, he blamed himself no less than Hitler for World War II. As Auden noted, the liturgy "uses we for the general confession, because each of us is in part responsible for the sins of our neighbors."

A monk lives a life of penance and prayer. One can do only as much as one can do. Merton lived the way he thought he ought to live, and thereby influenced the world. He complained in his journal about the 20th century, this "disgusting century: the century of poison gas and atomic bombs." He had gone off to join a monastery—not to escape from the world and its problems, but to join it to God through prayerful intercession. "My vocation," he wrote, "is prayer."

He became absorbed in the "ideas of the mythical and poetic expression of the doctrine of the 'fall' of man and original sin," he wrote to Rachel Carson, after reading her *Silent Spring*. (His fellow monks had been trying to exterminate bagworms at the monastery, but Carson's book persuaded them to give it up.) Man, he wrote, "has built into himself a tendency to destroy and negate himself when everything is at its best.... It is just when things are paradisiacal that he uses this power."

The 20th century was the most violent in the history of the world. Our technical prowess has allowed us to extend our violence to unprecedented lengths. At this writing–at the dawn of a new and troubling century–one-third of all nations in the world are involved in armed conflict. Terrorism is on the rise. Nuclear weaponry proliferates. The world is more dangerous now than at any other time in history.

We cannot, as Aldous Huxley warned, use evil means to attain a good end.

> Logic has ruined us,
> Theorems have flung their folly at us,
> Economy has left us full of swords
> And all our blood is gone...

Has progress turned out to be an illusion? Our technological advances have allowed us to kill people in more imaginative ways–this is the use to which we should put our collective imagination? Ought we to be suspicious of the inventions of our progress? Why, with all of our progress, are we not growing more peaceful? Why do our new technologies operate only within the old fears and paranoias? Why do we seem incapable of profound change?

X.

MERTON'S POEM about Nazi death camps, "Chant to Be Used in Processions Around a Site with Furnaces," refuses to allow any of us to escape responsibility for those atrocities. The poem is written in first person, so that the reader becomes the speaker, the death camp commandant:

> I was the commander I made improvements and installed a guaranteed system taking account of human weakness I purified and I remained decent

Stylistically, or anti-stylistically, the poem abandons lyrical shape for undifferentiated blocks of prose. It is a poem that – given its subject – cannot be typically "poetic." (I am also thinking here of the Frankfurt School-thinker Theodor Adorno's comment, "After the Holocaust, there can be no poetry.") Thematically, Merton implicates not only the Nazis; we are all part of that deadly circle, which widens treacherously over time. He anticipated such clinical modern warfare as the attacks in the computer-guided U.S. wars against Iraq, and he refuses to allow any of us absolution:

> Do not think yourself better because you burn up

friends and enemies with long-range missiles without ever seeing what you have done

Upon learning that the comic Lenny Bruce performed "Chant" in his nightclub act, Merton said, "People like Lenny Bruce are really monks in reverse" – which means, I suppose, someone who lives in the secular world and makes none of the sacrifices that a monk makes, but who is equally radical in his professed commitments.

Merton also used undifferentiated blocks of prose in his poem "Original Child Bomb." His account of the dropping of the first atomic weapon on Hiroshima forsakes poetic 'style' in order to describe the awful decision Truman made. Section 32 reads:

> The bomb exploded within 100 feet of the aiming point. The fireball was 18,000 feet across. The temperature at the center of the fireball was 100,000,000 degrees. The people who were near the center became nothing. The whole city was blown to bits and the ruins all caught fire instantly everywhere, burning briskly. 70,000 people were killed right away or died within a few hours. Those who did not die at once suffered great pain. Few of them were soldiers.

The Cold War madness of Mutually Assured Destruction (M.A.D.) fools no one anymore. It is madness. Numbers such as above, such as military strategists routinely use, numb the mind.

Merton is responding to such dreadnaught thinking as Herman Kahn's, a RAND intellectual in the 1950's specializing in such 'intellectual' areas as megadeath and throwweight. Kahn wrote, in his 1960 book *On Thermonuclear War,* "War is a terrible thing; but so is peace…." After a nuclear war, more babies have birth defects—but four percent of babies have birth defects anyway, he argued. "It might well turn out that U.S. decision-makers would be willing, among other things," he continued, "to accept this high risk of an additional one percent of our children being born deformed if that meant not giving up Europe to the Soviet Union." Imagine—this kind of thinking, from the man who is said to have the highest I.Q. ever recorded! Clearly, as Merton writes elsewhere, intelligence alone is not sufficient.

One of the American nicknames for the Hiroshima bomb was "Fat Boy." The Japanese called it "Original Child Bomb," because nothing like it had ever existed before. There is a terrible irony in their calling it a "child"—the *anti*-messiah come among us. Merton's poem is likewise ironic, in a deadpan way. Section 28:

> At the last minute before taking off, Col. Tibbetts changed the secret radio call sign from "Visitor" to "Dimples." The Bombing Mission would be a kind of flying smile.

Sixty atomic scientists who knew of the atomic bomb tests at Alamadorgo signed a petition, on July 21,

1945, saying this bomb should not be used against the Japanese without a significant warning and a chance to surrender. Their petition was ignored. Merton cites this petition in his poem, as well, and adds another grim little piece of history. Section 23:

> On August 2nd President Truman was the guest of His Majesty King George VI on board the H.M.S. Renown in Plymouth Harbor. The atomic bomb was praised. Admiral Leahy, who was present, declared that the bomb would not work. His Majesty George VI offered a small wager to the contrary.

Merton would later say that the West has technology without wisdom, and the East has wisdom without technology. Nowadays, the East has both wisdom and technology. Can the West claim to have both?

XI.

THE ROMAN POET VIRGIL spoke of the "iron sleep" of death. In his *Aeneid,* the Trojans solemnize the death of Anchises, saying (in John Dryden's translation),

"Dire dreams to thee, and iron sleep, he bears." Later in the poem, about a Trojan who lies slain, Virgil writes, "An iron sleep his stupid eyes oppressed." Iron—that inhuman element of warfare—echoes with the sound of woe.

Early in the 20th century, when everybody else was sporting straw boaters, the Kaiser Wilhelm went about wearing a metal-spiked helmet with an eagle on a blue background, in a not-so-subtle homage to Attila the Hun. The Imperial German post office issued a stamp bearing a profile of comely Germania corseted in an iron bosom! "When anger comes," Merton wrote in his poem "True Peril," "the sky is the color of armor."

Merton's early poem "The Flight into Egypt," about the cruel governor of Galilee, invokes Virgil's metaphor:

> Through every precinct of the wintry city
> Squadroned iron resounds upon the streets;
> Herod's police
> make shudder the dark steps of the tenements....

In the cadenced stomp of booted metal reverberate the thuddings of our own hearts in fear. Iron ringing underfoot—like the bombing practice at Fort Knox—terrifies as it goes about its hellish business. In another poem, "In Memory of the Spanish Poet Federico Garcia Lorca," the plaintive song of a woman mourning Lorca's assassination, by Franco's fascists, "has turned to iron in the naked air, / More loud and more despairing than a ruined tower."

Notice the lovely inversion Merton achieves, when the iron is turned inside-out, and becomes as supple, in the language of poetry, as a lady's handkerchief. The iron becomes a bell. How different from weaponry is the celebratory sound of church bells, whose essence is the airy tingling between peals! The metal has been hollowed out, and made hallowed, and a kind of silence calms our thudding hearts, like the silence Merton describes at the end of his poem "For My Brother: Reported Missing in Action, 1943":

> The silence of Whose tears shall fall
> Like bells upon your alien tombs.
> Hear them and come: they call you home.

Here is the sound of love, and of homecoming. In a poem about the abbey at sunrise (matins), Merton writes of the gloom of night, the "pilgrim" moon, hidden stars, and silence, all awakened by the call to morning prayers:

> ...from the frowning tower, the windy belfy,
> Sudden the bells come, bridegrooms,
> And fill the echoing dark with love and fear.
>
> *from "The Abbey of Gethsemani"*

There is every kind of difference between the iron of weaponry and the iron of bells—terror inverted, subverted into peace. The gentle reader is reminded of Bashō's old poem:

> The temple bell stops—
> but the sound keeps coming
> out of the flowers.
>
> (Robert Bly, trans.)

XII.

Denise Levertov, in her poem "Contraband," suggests that the "tree of knowledge was the tree of reason," but that it is "toxic in large quantities." Reason in excess, and the hubris that can come simply with knowing a lot, can become a tyranny of the mind, like a "dense cloud that harden[s] to steel." Or, as Gertrude Stein put it, in her 1959 essay *Reflections on the Atomic Bomb*, "Everybody gets so much information all day long that they lose their common sense." (And this was before the Internet!)

Reason and knowledge can wall us off from God, Merton says. Theology alone will not enable us to leap that wall—the leap of faith, that Miguel de Unamuno, the Spanish philosopher, first described. Merton wrote in his poem "Psalm:"

> When psalms surprise me with their music
> And antiphons turn to rum
> The Spirit sings….

How did he put it in his poem "Spring Storm"? He said "intellects go mumbling in the snow." What is needed is a letting-go – of knowledge, of striving, of old ways. ("Imagination," as Einstein said, "is more important than knowledge.") Again, from Merton's "Psalm:"

> And I go forth with no more wine and no more stars
> And no more buds and no more Eden
> And no more animals and no more sea:
>
> While God sings by Himself in acres of night
> And walls fall down, that guarded Paradise.

In the last year of his life, Merton wrote in his journal, "I wish I had done more creative work and less of this trivial, sanctimonious editorializing." Early on, he had written in a letter to his publisher, James Laughlin, "perhaps the most living way to approach theological and philosophical problems… [is] in the form of creative writing and literary criticism."

Clearly, Merton understood that any approach to God requires some creative thinking. Once stated, it does seem obvious. Why would one suppose that God can be approached dully, without imagination?

Poems and prayers are questions. They issue out of silence, into doubt, then return to silence once again.

I have always believed that it is not intellectual –

indeed, it is anti-intellectual—to say "I know." The mind is closed. But it is intellectual to say, "I do not know." The mind is open.

A question challenges. A question is the mode of the skeptic, the anti-authoritarian, the crank, the very one (the only one) who sometimes saves us from our excesses. In his "Letter to Pablo Antonio Cuadra Concerning Giants," Merton writes:

> I know it is not accepted as a sign of progressive thinking to question the enlightenment of the twentieth century barbarian. But I no longer have any desire to be considered enlightened by the standards of the stool pigeons and torturers whose most signal claim to success is that they have built so many extermination camps and operated them to the limit of their capacity.

As Rousseau is said to have remarked, What wisdom can you find that is greater than kindness?

XIII.

MERTON'S POETICAL ARGUMENT against war goes deeper than a mere protest against violence. He understood that war-mongering attitudes proceed from grave moral and ethical illness; they are a kind of insanity of the soul. "What concerns me, perhaps this is pride, is the ghastly feeling that we are all on the brink of a spiritual defection and betrayal of Christ," he wrote in a 1961 letter to Josiah Chatham, "which would consist in the complete acceptance of the values and decisions of the callous men of war who think only in terms of megacorpses and megatons, and have not the slightest thought for man, the image of God."

Merton worried about his own participation in that sort of misguided thinking. His grandfather had left him an inheritance that included stock in heavy industries, but the young Merton scarcely tapped it. "Wherever you have oil tanks or factories or railroads or any of the comforts of home and manifestations of progress in this country, you are sure to get bombers, sooner or later," he wrote in his journal. Imagine his relief, upon signing over his inheritance to Gethsemani when he walked through its doors! Over its gate, of course, the inscription *Pax Intrantibus:* Peace to Those Who Enter. "I am scared to own anything," he continued in that same journal entry, "even a name, let alone a coin or shares in oil, the munitions, the airplane factories. I am scared to take a proprietary interest in anything for fear that my love of what I own may be killing somebody somewhere."

Why is warfare wrong?

If we could put the question bluntly to Merton, I

imagine he might have said: "Man is made in the image of God; killing man kills God.

"A monk practices humility. Humility means trying not to offend God. Warfare is wrong because it offends God."

XIV.

In 1958 Merton wrote a sort of fan letter to Czeslaw Milosz. He had just read Milosz's *The Captive Mind*, the now-classic study of the social psychology of communism. "Your book has come to me as something I can frankly call 'spiritual,'" Merton wrote, "that is to say as the inspiration of much thought, meditation and prayer about my own obligations to the rest of the human race, and about the predicament of us all....

"Is there anything I can do for you? It seems to me that the most obvious thing I can give you is the deep and friendly interest of a kindred mind and a will disposed for receptiveness and collaboration. And, of course, my prayers."

Their letters over the next decade, until Merton's

death in 1968, explored their common ground of political acuity, social angst and spiritual questing. In a later book, *The Witness of Poetry,* Milosz wrote that, if one were to look about for a reasoned explanation of the horrors that have been visited on the 20th century, no other possibility remains but to agree with the Epicureans that either the gods are omnipotent but not very good, or they are good but not omnipotent. Either way, literature is a way of doing something. In a poem from 1945, Milosz asks, "What is poetry which does not save nations or people?"

Yes, writing can do only so much. Merton and Milosz shared a particular writerly frustration. "You are right to feel a certain shame about writing," Merton wrote, in 1959. "I do too, but always too late – five years after a book has appeared, I wish I had never been such a fool as to write it. But when I am writing it, I think it is good. If we were not all fools we would never accomplish anything at all." Milosz was not one to rue earlier work; he famously acknowledged what he considered to be his limitations, and he let his poems stand as mile-markers along that long and wearying road, bounded, on the one side, by uncertainty, and, on the other, by desire. Milosz lived at the crossroads of the 19th and 20th centuries; Rome and Byzantium; East and West; the life of the flesh and the life of the mind. His lovely poem "On Prayer" begins, "You ask me how to pray to someone who is not," and, ever nimble with paradox, he concludes:

Notice: I say we; there, every one separately,
Feels compassion for others entangled in the flesh
And knows that if there is no other shore
We will walk that aerial bridge all the same.

"My constant problem," Milosz wrote to Merton in 1961, "I believe, with a part of myself (in which resides poetry and meditation on the precariousness of space-time), in the Incarnation, the Resurrection, and the resurrection of the body. I cannot believe in the immortality of the soul." Milosz also had trouble with the traditional representations of the Savior. In his poem "Sentences," which Merton published in his literary journal *Monks Pond*, Milosz wrote:

Perhaps we should have represented him otherwise
Than in the form of a dove. As fire, yes,…beyond us
For even when it consumes logs on a hearth
We search in it for eyes and hands. Let him then be…
Blowing a birchbark trumpet so strongly that
      farther down
There tumbles from its blast a crowd of petty officials,
Their uniforms unbuttoned and their women's combs
Flying like chips when the ax strikes.

XV.

In anticipation of milosz's 1999 visit to Bellarmine University, where I teach, I stocked my freezer with some very good and expensive Polish vodka. We did not drink much of it. Only Milosz and our academic dean Theresa Sandok (also Polish) had the constitution to imbibe the stuff. The next day I asked Milosz, would the vodka be harmed if I removed it from my freezer? He turned to me and grumbled in that deeply accented voice of his, "Vodka's indestructible."

Perhaps that is why vodka is the drink of choice in so many troubled nations of Eastern Europe – its conferred indestructibility.

Milosz survived Stalinist repression to become a poet of social and political engagement. Even as his poems take history into account, they also transcend history, and become, themselves, exemplars of his own brave comment:

Human reason is beautiful and invincible.
No bars, no barbed wire, no pulping of books,
No sentence of banishment can prevail against it.
It puts what should be above things as they are.
It does not know Jew from Greek nor slave from master.

What can poetry do? Of Milosz's lines just above,

Seamus Heaney wrote, in an essay for the *New York Times*:

> It is thrilling to hear the ideal possibilities of human life stated so unambiguously and unrepentantly. For a moment, the dirty slate of history seems to have been wiped clean. The lines return us to the bliss of beginnings. They tempt us to credit all over again liberations promised by the Enlightenment and harmonies envisaged by the scholastics, to believe that the deep well of religious and humanist value may still be unpolluted.

Milosz's earliest poems announced a poet of keen intellectual curiosity. His poem "Encounter," from 1936, describes riding through frozen fields in a wagon at dawn, a rabbit dashing across the road, someone's hand pointing, and concludes:

O my love, where are they, where are they going,
The flash of a hand, streak of movement, rustle of pebbles.
I ask not out of sorrow, but in wonder.

That significant distinction—"not out of sorrow, but in wonder"—introduced to the world a poet of soulful openness.

On which point, I think, he and Merton are brothers. After getting permission to stay nights at his hermitage (built by undergraduate boys from Bellarmine), Merton wrote in his journal, for October 20, 1964, "Sleeping here has been a great grace. Last night, full moon. At midnight the whole valley was drenched in silence and dark clarity."

Dark clarity. Now there's a phrase that Milosz might have written. Does it amount to "wonder"? I see a deep mystery in many of Merton's poems, perhaps most succinctly in this little untitled poem:

> All of the branches
> None of the roots.
> > All of the words–
> > Freedom branches
> > All of the words
> > Happiness branches
> > All of the words
> > Equality branches
> > None of the roots.
> All of the branches
> None of the roots.

XVI.

AUDEN SAID POETRY makes nothing happen (though he maintained that liturgy does). But he knew this not to be true. His poem, "9 September, 1931," which he later repudiated, held the now-famous line, "We must love one another or die." Readers embraced this line, and were enacting it in their own lives, and using it as a call to action. Perhaps Auden was a bit taken aback. What is this line if not a plea to save people, in Milosz's phrase?

Poetry is one form of prayer. Or, if you prefer, prayer is one form of poetry. "Poetry at its best is contemplation," Mark van Doren has written, "of things, and of what they signify. Not what they can be made to signify, but what they actually do signify, even when nobody knows it." The poet, like the monk, can work to pull the world to safety.

Words are things. A poem is an act. In ancient China, for example, poetry was the language of the court, and an event–birth, death, love affair, appointment, business transaction–was not complete until a poem had been written about it. The poem completed the event. Bashō, on his trek into the deep north of Japan, wrote haiku along the way to mark his journey –to make it real. When Merton visited Chobgye Thiccen Rinpoche in Dharamsala, in the Himalayas, they talked, and, as he wrote in his journal on November 7, 1968, "He seemed very pleased and wrote a poem for me. I wrote one for him." This is very Zen, the formalizing of a visit with poems written on the spot, upon the occasion.

It was, in fact, Catholic Jesuits who first brought Buddhism to the world's attention. The Jesuits traveled widely, especially in the 17th and 18th centuries. It was not in their habit to preach without also learning and respecting the local religions. They incorporated many native American traditions into their mission service in California, for one example. Those Jesuits who traveled to China listened closely to their Buddhist brethren, and they translated and commented upon many Buddhist texts.

The Dalai Lama named Merton a Catholic *geshe*. There exists perhaps no higher honor. It is a kind of honorary doctorate, conferred by the most enlightened among us. And it is conferred not on the basis of intellect, or training, but on the basis of character. Merton's translation of Chuang Tzu's poem "The Man of Tao" begins:

> The man in whom Tao
> Acts without impediment
> Harms no other being
> By his actions
> Yet he does not know himself
> To be "kind," to be "gentle."

XVII.

ZEN IS ABOUT CHARACTER, not intellect. An illiterate woodcutter can be a poet-monk of the first order, as long as his character is right. And so it was: Hui Neng, of the early T'ang dynasty in China, a woodcutter who could neither read nor write, declared in his *Platform Sutras,* "The complete teachings of all Buddhas past, present and future–are to be found within the essence of every human being." Ability–like the soul –is indwelling.

Does the poet will his work into being? Or, is poetry visited upon only the worthy?

"Meaning is not something we impose," Merton wrote, "but a mystery which we can discover." Literature teachers are trained to teach literature. They are readers of literature who know how to share with students the ways to receive literary works into their full selves. Such teachers are often the very ones who awaken in students a desire to write. But, unless these teachers are also poets, or fiction writers themselves, they tend to teach creative writing (if at all) by the only means they know–as a working backward from literature. They tend to emphasize forms, and the ideas for assignments, rather than the open-ended discovery which describes writing at its best.

Writers know that form emerges from the writing. To borrow an adage from architects, *Form follows function*. And, in writing, function is rarely clear at the outset. One cannot begin with form, except in the most mechanistic way, and it does not guarantee–in fact, it fairly precludes–good writing. U.S. Poet Laureate Ted Kooser writes, in the *Poetry Home Repair*

Manual, "Every successful sonnet is a good poem first and a good sonnet second."

Writers also know that one cannot begin with ideas. Poems and stories issue from characters and images. Like form, the idea(s) must emerge. Writing is an act of discovery for the writer–neither the outcome nor its meaning can be predetermined.

In a sense, each of Merton's poems is a mystery discovered. We know that poems simply "came" to Merton. La Caridad handed him his first poem, but he was also ready to receive it. The groundwork for his poetry (as well as his conversion) had been well-prepared. About his poem "Elegy for the Monastery Barn," for example, Merton wrote in the preface to *The Strange Islands* (1957), the poem was written as one of the barns at Gethsemani burned down. "The monks left meditation to fight a very hot fire, but the poem arrived about the same time as the fire truck...." It was, he said, a beautiful fire.

> Laved in the flame as in a Sacrament
> The brilliant walls are holy
> In their first-last hour of joy.

The great Romanian poet Lucian Blaga believed poetry means to deepen the mystery of the world. Science will explain the world to us, but poetry is not about explanation. To welcome that mystery onto the page takes a fellow of a certain character. The American poet William Stafford used to get up very early in the morning and sit beside a window, waiting for the day to bring him a poem. His job? To make himself ready and worthy. To be receptive.

"Poems mostly write themselves," the Serbian-American poet Charles Simic has written. "Metaphors and similes owe everything to chance. A poet cannot will a memorable comparison. These things just pop into somebody's head."

Readiness is all.

In his journal for the second Sunday in Lent, Merton wrote, "In a Zen koan someone said that an enlightened man is not one who seeks Buddha or finds Buddha, but just an ordinary man who has *nothing left to do*." Perhaps this is what giving up the world is meant to accomplish. Solitude is a deepening of the present moment, attaining a full presence in the moment. This, too, seems very Zen.

Daisetz Suzuki said Merton was the one Westerner who understood Zen better than any other.

XVIII.

THE POET'S JOB IS not to speak, but to listen, so that things will speak through him. Po Chu-I wrote ten thousand poems. Shotetsu wrote thirty thousand! Issa wrote a thousand poems just about insects. Hurrah, we say – they listened well!

Silence laps at the poem's every edge. Like meditation, like prayer, poetry is surrounded by silence and is composed of silences, like the silences in between notes of a symphony. A poem is made of words, yes, but take away the words and poetry still remains, said Yang Wan-li a thousand years ago.

Writers I know seek out the silences of such places as Gethsemani and St. Meinrad abbeys, where the quiet is noted by the silver tones of bells calling out the progress of the day. The bells generally begin rather promptly every morning, ringing the Angelus at 6 a.m.

"A single stroke of the early prayer-bell wakes me," Tu Fu wrote. "Does it also waken my soul?"

Silence is a rich field. Walk out into a meadow. Sit down and be silent. The silence feels immense. (We are not used to being silent.) Then, slowly, you become aware of little sounds. Rustlings of leaves. Insects in the grass. All the sounds that would have remained unknown to you, had you not gone silent for a while.

"In silence," Merton wrote, "we face and admit the gap between the depths of our being, which we consistently ignore, and the surface which is untrue to our own reality."

The accomplishment of silence is wisdom. Silence is not an absence, but a presence, as we mentioned earlier, and perhaps it may also be a passage through knowledge into a greater awareness. Merton's poem "Wisdom" explicates the point:

> I studied it and it taught me nothing.
> I learned it and soon forgot everything else:
> Having forgotten, I was burdened with knowledge—
> The insupportable knowledge of nothing.
>
> How sweet my life would be, if I were wise!
> Wisdom is well known
> When it is no longer seen or thought of.
> Only then is understanding bearable.

Silence is another country, a place apart, hospitable and green, where you will be taken in, bathed and fed, and where your name—your true name—is spoken by the flowers. Like illness, silence has its own rules, which are nowhere written down, yet must be followed.

There can be a wrong silence, though, like the wrong resurrection that Merton identified in his poem about the guns of Fort Knox. When he writes of the neutron bomb, he is writing of such a perversion:

> ...I hear they are working on a bomb that will destroy nothing but life. Men, animals, birds, perhaps also vegetation. But it will leave buildings, factories, railways, natural resources. Only one further step, and the weapon will be one of absolute perfection. It should also destroy books, works of art,

musical instruments, toys, tools and gardens....

> "A Letter to Pablo Antonio Cuadra
> Concerning Giants"

XIX.

For a time, in the 1960's, Merton's superiors silenced his work. They deemed it unseemly for a Catholic monk to publish personal meditations—detailed accounts of his travails in the world of the spirit. They also deemed it unseemly for a monk to proclaim on political matters, such as the undeclared war in Vietnam. But, when they lifted the ban (the eminent French philosopher Jacques Maritain had earlier intervened on his behalf), Merton jumped right back into the fray. Whether his subject was war, racism, or other social issues, his message was consistent: nonviolence. When asked to write about humility, by the German pacifist Hildegaard Goss-Mayr, Merton said he would do so but only "in the context of nonviolence." His article for her, "Blessed Are the Meek: The Christian Roots of Nonviolence," (later collected in *Passion for Peace: The Social Essays*), concludes:

> The Christian, in his humility and faith, must be as totally available to his brother, to his world, in the present, as the child is. But he cannot see the world with childlike innocence and simplicity unless his memory is cleared of past evils by forgiveness, and his anticipation of the future is hopefully free of craft and calculation. For this reason, the humility of Christian nonviolence is at once patient and uncalculating. The chief difference between nonviolence and violence is that the latter depends entirely on its own calculations. The former depends entirely on God and on His Word.

Nonviolence is a vaunted ideal, but has been made state policy only one time in human history, to my knowledge—Ashoka, the Indian king during the time of the Buddha, became so taken with young Gautama's message that he embraced nonviolence by governmental decree. Certainly, Europe's adventure in the Americas had been predicated on violence. And, unfortunately, America's adventures in the Muslim world these days seem to be equally violent. A note of restraint, anyone?

Merton's poetry made a rare appearance in the U.S. House of Representatives, on April 12, 1962, when his poem "Prayer for Peace" was read aloud, and it included these lines:

Grant us prudence in proportion to our power,
Wisdom in proportion to our science,
Humaneness in proportion to our wealth and might.

XX.

We have seen that violence can lie near to the religious heart. Just a few years after the Trappist brothers from France established their monastery at Gethsemani, anti-Catholic riots broke out in Louisville. On Bloody Monday–August 6, 1855–Protestant mobs killed at least twenty-two Catholics, inflamed by propaganda demonizing Catholics as members of a sexually perverse, treasonous conspiracy intent on taking over America for the Pope. Other cities suffered anti-Catholic attacks. Much of the ire was fueled by anti-immigrant sentiment, a view held by Louisville's newspaper editor at the time. August 6 was an election day. Protestant mobs bullied immigrants away from the polls, then began rioting in predominantly German and Irish neighborhoods. The Armbruster brewery was burned. (I suppose there was no imported beer yet–would the rioters have imbibed?) Mobs threatened to attack two cathedrals, St. Martin of Tours and Cathedral of the Assumption, claiming Catholics used them to store weapons; the churches were spared only when the mayor himself inspected the buildings and declared them free of weapons caches. The day after Bloody Monday, Catholic and Protestant leaders alike appealed for calm—not revenge.

XXI.

We have seen too much sectarian violence. In our own time this has proliferated: Arab and Jew, Anglican and Catholic, Protestant and Muslim, et cetera. Seamus Heaney once told me about meeting Irish Republican Army political leader Gerry Adams in a Dublin pub. Two such world figures cannot exactly ignore each other in a small space. Adams came over and shook the laureate's hand, whereupon Seamus went directly to the men's room and "washed my hands clean of the blood of my countrymen."

Clearly, what the world needs is an enlightened ecumenism, such as Merton evinced in his embrace of Buddhism and other faith traditions, most intriguingly Sufism, the ecstatic, mystical aspect of Islam. It is easy to see how Sufism appealed to him. In his *Asian Journal,* Merton identified its objective: "to gain knowledge of and communion with God through contemplation." Sufism is interested not so much in doctrine as in direct spiritual experience. Those Sufi mystics most familiar to the West are the whirling dervishes, who can spin for hours and levitate in their religious fervor.

Merton's interest in Islam, scholar Bonnie Thurston has written, "like his interest in Buddhism, tended to be focused on its mystical traditions.... But the world and culture of Islam was also very much in Merton's bloodstream. The transfusion came by means of his European roots, his 'French connection,' if you will, and his knowledge of Romance languages. But the result was very much Islamic and not European, which is to say Merton embraced Islam, not some European Orientalist's version of it."

Merton read Martin Lings, Herbert Mason and Titus Burchhardt on Sufism. He read Avicenna and Ibn-Arabi. He also read Rumi, the Persian mystic poet, in whose writings are united the traditions of Mohammed and Christ. Like Merton, Rumi was a poet first, an apostle second. (The Persians called him Jelaluddin Balkhi.) At the beginning of each chapter of his *Mathnawi,* Rumi put a poem-prayer. He found that poetry best expressed his soul's nature, and, for him (as for Merton), poetry navigates the middle path between silence and speech:

> There is a way between voice and presence
> where information flows.
> In disciplined silence it opens.
> With wandering talk it closes.

Rumi wrote Jesus poems. Merton wrote Buddha poems. Some say that Jesus Himself spent time among Muslim and Buddhist monks. Such cross-fertilization would underscore the basic agreements between the world's great religions: the search for God, peaceableness, and hospitality. Why is it important to welcome the stranger into your midst, beyond the thought that he represents Christ, or the Buddha? Rumi wrote:

> Be grateful for whoever comes,
> because each has been sent
> as a guide from beyond.

In his lectures to the novices at Gethsemani, Merton spoke about the Sufi understanding of contemplation, which he paraphrased as "simple openness to God at every moment, and deep peace." To me, the most important word there is "simple." It does not admit sectarian differences, nor scholastic liturgical argument. As Rumi wrote:

> Christ is the population of the world,
> and every object as well. There is no room
> for hypocrisy. Why use bitter soup for healing
> when sweet water is everywhere?

Buddhists say that all creatures, and all things, have

Buddha-nature. Rumi said that all creatures and things have Christ-nature. Dare a Christian, in these times, say that all creatures and things have Allah-nature?

Bonnie Thurston concludes an essay in *The Merton Seasonal,* "Islam in Alaska: Sufi Material in *Thomas Merton in Alaska,*" with this wistful thought: "Perhaps had God granted Merton to remain with us, we should have been able to appreciate more fully the beauties of Islamic spirituality, been spared the sin of demonizing it and destroying countries and cultures in which it flourishes."

XXII.

Merton wrote poems of Islam. What a marvelous thing! His turning to Sufism marked a radical ecumenism, as radical as Rumi's and Christ's. Merton's poem "The Night of Destiny" observes the end of Ramadan, the Moslem fast, and the giving of the Koran to Mohammed, when the heavens are opened and the Holy Words are heard on earth. This poem concludes:

> Only in the Void
> Are all ways one:
>
> Only in the night
> Are all the lost
> Found.
>
> In my ending is my meaning.

A former student of mine, who became an advertising executive representing a famous soft-drink company, tells a harrowing story concerning Ramadan. He recalls a meeting where the corporate officers were lamenting the world-wide drop in soft-drink consumption during Ramadan, and, while discussing new advertising strategies, one officer declared, "We want to *own* Ramadan!" At that point, my student left the room, eventually gave up the business, and took a teaching position in advertising ethics at Virginia Tech University.

What is the chief sin here? Lack of hospitality, I think. The holy holiday of Ramadan was supremely unimportant to soft-drink executives. "The desecration, de-sacralization of the modern world is manifest above all by the fact that the stranger is of no account," Merton wrote in "A Letter to Pablo Antonio Cuadra Concerning Giants." Certainly, these days, the Muslim is the extreme stranger in the West. (And, increasingly, Westerners are strangers in the Muslim world.) Merton continued, "There is more than one way of morally liquidating the 'stranger' and the 'alien.' It is sufficient to destroy, in some way, that in him which is different and disconcerting. By pressure, persuasion, or force one can impose on him one's own ideas and attitudes towards life. One can indoctrinate him, brainwash him." When religious sensibilities are subverted to corporate interests—when the whole world drinks American soft-drinks—there is no need to seek any higher reality, or so the advertisements tell us.

Allen Ginsberg said the U.S.A. stood for the United States of Advertising. Ginsberg also asked, in his poem "America"—"America, when will you look at yourself through the grave?" What life, America, do you want to end up with? When Merton gave up his grandfather's Wall Street stocks, deeding them over to the monastery, he hoped to shed himself of the mercenary corporate thinking that tries, daily, to take over the world in the name of commerce.

XXIII.

FORTY YEARS AGO, when the U.S. was bombing a small Buddhist country (Vietnam) "back into the stone age," as one General LeMay promised, Merton wrote these words in a letter to Abdul Aziz, the Pakistani Muslim scholar:

> Well, my friend, we live in troubled and sad times, and we must pray the infinite and merciful Lord to bear patiently with the sins of this world, which are very great. We must humble our hearts in silence and poverty of spirit and listen to His commands which come from the depths of His love, and work that men's hearts may be converted to the ways of love and justice, not of blood, murder, lust and greed. I am afraid that the big powerful countries are a very bad example to the rest of the world in this respect.

As of this writing, the U.S. is bombing a small Muslim country (Iraq) into "shock and awe," as one Pentagon official promised. (What are we to think, now that our use of murder to improve the world comes complete with marketing slogans?) Islam means not peace, as some have suggested, but submission–submission to the will of Allah, who is a peace-loving deity. What modern deity preaches war?

Merton instructed the novices at Gethsemani for many years, and much of his poem "Readings from Ibn Abbad" is dedicated to his novices. "8: To a Novice" concludes:

> Be a son of this instant,
> Thanking Allah
> For a mouthful of ashes.

Sufism represents not only mystic enlightenment, but also the way of poverty. Poverty is a gift that frees us from the need for material things. Albert Camus, in his notebook for May 1935, wrote, "One can, without romanticism, feel nostalgic for lost poverty. A certain number of years lived without money are enough to create a whole sensibility." Camus grew up in Algeria, the sunny north coast of Africa, and so what need had he of money? He had the sun, the sea, and a boyhood eternity of time, and he was perhaps never happier in his life.

After visiting a Franciscan cloister in San Francisco, Camus wrote about "an extreme point at which poverty always rejoins the luxury and richness of the world. If they cast everything off, it is for a great and not for another life."

Franciscans follow the rule of St. Francis, of course, who as a young man renounced his father's riches. His father sought recourse in the courts, where the son stripped himself naked to make a point of his renunciation. An aide to the court rushed out and found a rough, brown woolen cloak to hide the boy's nakedness, and that has been the Franciscans' garb ever since.

If ashes are all you have to eat, then eat ashes. If this moment is all that you inhabit, then inhabit it. And thank Allah, for these ashes, for this moment.

XXIV.

Writers and artists inhabit a kind of imaginary society. A poet has more in common with another poet, in another part of the world, than he has with his actual neighbor. Merton wrote of this. His correspondence with Boris Pasternak seemed both "strange and marvelous" to him, and he commented to Frater Lawrence about this "apparently easy and natural communication between a monk in a strictly guarded Trappist monastery and a suspect poet behind the Iron Curtain. I am in closer contact with Pasternak than I am with people in Louisville or Bardstown or even in my own monastery. I have more in common with him."

Some years ago, the Hungarian-born painter known simply as Batuz founded the Societie Imaginiere. The society has no headquarters, no dues, no rules of order. But it does have nearly 500 "members"—writers, artists, and scholars from around the world. Occasionally they come together to drink and dine, talk and exchange ideas. Though not a joiner, Merton, I think, would have liked this group.

Writers from the old Eastern bloc nations tend to see such communion as a triumph of creative will over politics. Western writers, who have traditionally enjoyed greater civil and artistic freedoms, find that they must bridge a growing cultural isolation, spurred by the mass media and a corporate culture. Nonetheless, by reading each other's work, and through correspondence, an intellectual community is formed that overcomes geographical and geopolitical boundaries.

Culturally, Merton saw himself as a citizen of the world. In addition to his voluminous correspondence, he also translated poems from Spanish, Latin, French, Portuguese, Chinese, Greek, Persian, et cetera. One does not need to know all these languages in order to make translations, of course; one can triangulate the language and write a respectable interpretation. His "Tomb Cover of Iman Riza" is a version of a translation by A.J. Arberry of an inscription on a cloth once laid over the tomb of the Iman, which Merton saw on a visit to the Cincinnati Art Museum in 1960. It reads, in part:

Here is the threshold of holiness in the dust of the road
 where mighty kings have laid their heads and crowns
Men and spirits, birds and beasts, fairies and demons
 all have laid their heads down in the court of
 His presence.
No wonder that they lay the head of service and obedience
 on the threshold of Him descended from the prophet
For having laid the hand of seeking on the skirt of Haidar
 their desire is fulfilled

Seeking for grace the holy cherubim have spread
 their pinions under the footsteps of His visitors.

The important thing, I think, is to note Merton's ecumenical spirit. Soon enough we shall be dispersed, Merton seemed to say, in an untitled poem from 1964:

> Things and people goodbye
> It is not that I prefer
> The singleness of death
> Where no companions are,
> Yet things and "you" and "I"
> The "he" the "she" the "they"
> Must all go off alone
> In common, not to be–
> And not in company.

–and so, while we are yet here a while, let's have a communion.

Merton's gregarious sociability cut against his deep desire for solitude, and indeed his monastic orders, but he could not help himself. His letters fill volumes. As he gained from the abbey an increasing freedom to travel, he wrote, in the last year of his life,

> The old monk is turned loose
> And can travel!
> He's out to see the world.
> What progress in the last thirty years!
> But his mode of travel
> Is still the same.

Then he turned, and, for his friend Robert Lax who was pointing a camera, he made a goofy face.

XXV.

Merton's last book (actually a manuscript he left unfinished), *The Geography of Lograire,* references the pine forests around his hermitage. He was Thomas of the Woods, as surely as Villon was Francois des Loges. And, in the kingdom of Lograire, every boy is named Francis. As Merton wrote in a prefatory author's note, "A poet spends his life in repeated projects, over and over attempting to build or to dream the world in which he lives. But more and more he realizes that this world is at once his and everybody's."

A poem has its own logic, but is not logically made; thus, to attempt an interpretation by logic misses the mark. As poet Charles Simic has noted, one cannot approach the achievement of poetry with the language of criticism. Poetry does, however, have its methods. So, we cannot talk about what a poem means (in John Ciardi's old but trusty formulation) so much as how the poem means. And in *Geography*, Merton bursts the bonds of liturgy—"these poems incidentally are never explicitly theological," he claims, "or even metaphysical"–to achieve an unmediated language that re-dreams creation. Though he speaks of the Lamb and holy walks and Cain, Geography is a dream-book, and these religious images are equal to kayaks and biscuits and ducks–figments of the same dream, wafting through its pages.

How to understand–how even to read–this book, with passages such as this?

8. Wet street. Change. Ring Cincinnati. Wake daycolor. Neosubstance comes to life in hospital. She makes wide frightwindows. Haze. Southward goes the sun.

Indeed, the poet interjects, just a few pages further on, IF YOU HAVE HEART FAILURE WHILE READING THIS / THE POET IS NOT RESPONSIBLE. It is like a dialect, this language. It is the dialect of Lograire. If the reader submits to it, the language begins to come clear, like a stream un-muddying itself before the patient reader.

Merton was not concerned with piety but with ascension. (He never campaigned to be abbot.) He sought a literary equivalent to ecstatic spiritual mysticism. He found it in the mythical forests of Lograire. His "A Clever Stratagem: Or, How to Handle Mystics," explains, by way of allegory:

> When I was out in the Nyasaland Missions we held a meeting of five thousand converts at which religious fervor naturally mounted to the highest pitch. So much intensity of religious

feeling required to be carefully channeled to prevent outbursts. Fervor must not be permitted to dissipate itself in wasteful, even riotous disorders. One morning two of the leading teachers came to report some experiences they were having. They had been out in the bush all night praying and they had felt their bodies lifted up from the earth while bright angelic beings came to meet them as they ascended. What did this mean? I replied not in words but in deed. I went to the dispensary, took down the salts, gave them each a stiff dose and sent them off to bed. The visions and ascensions immediately ceased, and were replaced by a sweetly reasonable piety that disturbed no one. A missionary must combine spiritual passion with sound sense. He must keep an eye on his followers.

So, when in *Geography of Lograire* Merton writes

TEN GUNS ARE OUT OF WORK UP ANGER HOLLOW

Try outsmart Saturday night's air
Tight teller sees city split where
Manmade bloodrains light and chemistry wet
Upon blue grass signs the red flower forever

he is finding an intensity of language to match an intensity of feeling.

The French logos refers to little huts used by woodcutters—and which remind us of the huts inhabited by Buddhist monks, prized for their rusticity. There is much that Merton shares with the great Chinese poet-monks of antiquity. They flourished during western Europe's Dark Ages, creating a high culture of poetry and art, while Europeans were still slaughtering each other for the price of a roasted boar. The Chinese poet-monks praised nonviolence and transcendence. They forsook grander lodgings for simple hermitages and a more direct experience of the universe. Above all, they prized a simple life – a life lived at the level of essentials, so as not to clutter the enlightenment-seeking mind. If the roof leaked, and moonlight – delicious, milk-white moonlight – shone through, so much the better.

XXVI.

The trappist monks at Gethsemani make and sell cheese and fruitcakes, in order to support the abbey. In Merton's time, the brother who operated the printing press (used primarily for cheese labels) was also inveighed upon to print Merton's literary journal, *Monks Pond*. This circumstance presented Merton with some challenges. When one young poet, Geof Hewitt, submitted a poem with some sexual content, Merton returned it, saying:

> You sense my problem: in detail, it is this: the devout young monk who runs the offset machine for me can cause trouble for me and all my pomps and works by simply refusing to cooperate, denouncing me to the authorities, etc etc. Now I am sure he thinks rubbers are something that go on your feet and has not sufficient experience of the world to wonder how they cost so little. But he does know that bullshit is dirty.

Monks Pond ran as an entirely underground operation. By design, no money changed hands, the magazine was sent free to those who expressed an interest, and there was no advertising or promotion. Furthermore, Merton had no particular editorial program. *Monks Pond* published experimental poetry (such as concrete poetry and antipoetry) and political lyrics, as well as ecological and spiritual work. Merton's literary interests were as ecumenical as his spiritual interests. He wrote, in a letter to the poet Margaret Randall, "Need poems, prose, ideas, anything so long as it doesn't get me burned by the monks. If it is something they don't figure out OK...."

He published work by anti-poeticist Nicanor Parra, Otto René Castillo, the French poet Robert Desnos, Milosz, Jonathan Williams, Ted Enslin, Robert Lax, Kerouac, and even the German painter Paul Klee:

> To invent
> the Chorus Mysticus
> to be performed
> by a few hundred
> children's voices
>
> After that
> no need to go on
> with the constant endeavor
>
> The many small works
> all lead to it
> in the end.
>
> (Anselm Hollo, trans.)

Merton also published a remarkable short poem by Wendell Berry, entitled "February 2, 1968," which reads, in its entirety:

> In the dark of the moon, in flying snow, in the dead of winter,
> war spreading, families dying, the world in danger,
> I walk the rocky hillside, sowing clover.

Clover is a plant whose seed is best sown during a winter snowfall. The snow gives the seed moisture, and eases it into the ground so the birds don't eat it. Sowing clover is also an act of hope. Scholar Bert Hornback has commented, "When I put the first line together with the third line, I see a farmer doing what he must do in cooperation with nature. When I put the second and third lines together, I see what anyone must do, in active protest against the unnatural things going on in this world."

Merton froze the *Pond* over after one year. As an editor, he was frequently overwhelmed, distracted, unorganized. But that describes many editors of literary journals, who do their work not for money, but for the love of literature. It's a good thing the abbey didn't count on the journal for any income.

All monasteries need a livelihood. Sometimes they must cope with unusual circumstances—even successes, like the healthy royalties from Merton's best-selling autobiography, *Seven Storey Mountain,* for example. The thirty or so monks at the Abbey of St. Sixtus of Westvleteven, in Flanders, for another example, brew beer. Beer enthusiasts from sixty-five countries voted recently the monks' dry, dark Westvleteven 12 the world's best beer, on the Website RateBeer.com. Unfortunately for all concerned, the beer's sudden popularity depleted the abbey's supply. "Our shop is closed because all our beer has been sold out," said a message on the abbey's answering machine.

XXVII.

M‍erton is a large figure. Every reader has his or her own Merton. How can there be only one Merton?

> *Though appearing to act he does not engage in action*
> "Geography of Lograire"

His character, as expressed in his voluminous writings, is perhaps best defined by questioning, struggle, ambiguity and paradox. "It must have been a contest all his life, between retreat and attack," his friend Lawrence Ferlinghetti said. Merton's attitude toward his own legacy seems equally muddied. Merton disavowed his one best-selling book, his *Seven Storey Mountain,* and he described the Merton Room at the Bellarmine University library as "a good place to cut a fart and run." He also wrote, in his journal, of his "pretended 'roots' at Gethsemani, where I am alien and where most everyone else is too. Yet paradoxically to many people I am completely identified with this strange place I can't firmly believe in." To this emerging cipher, we must add the mysterious element of his creative genius. Such a thing as creative genius can never be explained.

> *His actions in this world are appearances only*

Even in his Catholicity he is difficult to pin down. He claims to have seen no contradiction between Catholicism and Buddhism, for example. While it is one thing to say, as he did in Bangkok, that he wanted to be the best Buddhist he could be, it is quite another thing to say, as he did earlier, that he wanted to be a Jew to Jews, a Hindu to Hindus, a Buddhist to Buddhists, et cetera, because what does that mean? And, in respect to changes in the church, Merton considered himself neither a progressive nor a traditionalist.

He who sees reality in the universe may try to negate it

So, Merton is a known quantity and also an unknown quantity.

Prankster. Priest. Smiling hillbilly. Bongos. Calligrapher. Pines. Beer. Activist. Teacher. Seer-mystic. Cheese. Editor. Epiphany. Solitude. Poet.

XXVIII.

In my ending is my meaning

In 1968, Merton met with the Dalai Lama, in Dharamsala, and they affirmed a brotherly connection. They spoke of Tibetan Buddhism and Western monasticism, among many other subjects, and "at the end I felt we had become very good friends," Merton wrote in his journal, "and were somehow quite close to each other."

That evening, the lights in Merton's cottage went dead for a minute. He wandered outside and looked up at the moon–a Zen symbol of transcendence–and listened to the echoing of drums from the village below. "The same constellations as over the hermitage," back in Kentucky, he wrote. The porch of his Dharamsala cottage opened in the same direction as his Gethsemani hermitage, southeast toward the constellations Aquita and the Dolphin. That night, he dreamed that he was:

> back at Gethsemani. I was dressed in a Buddhist monk's habit, but with more black and red and gold, a "Zen habit," in color more Tibetan than Zen. I was going to tell Brother Donald, the cook in the diet kitchen, that I would be there for supper. I met some women in the corridor, visitors and students of Asian religion, to whom I was explaining I was a kind of Zen monk and *Gelugpa* together, when I woke up.

Over the next several weeks, Merton traveled by plane, Land-rover, train and boat to Darjeeling, Calcutta, Bagdogra, Kanchenjunga, Madras, Colombo, Singapore, Bangkok.... Ever aware, I imagine, of the ancient Buddhist concept of *anicca*–impermanence.

In his destination city of Bangkok, he spoke to an ecumenical conference about the connections between

Catholicism and Buddhism. His talk was not particularly well-received. He tried, too much for some, to reconcile the world's religious differences. A noble impulse, and an impossible task. Anyway, Merton delivered the lecture, then retired to his room. He had been profoundly moved by the spirituality of the Tibetans he met; perhaps, that afternoon he had a poem in his head–some lines about prayer flags, incense, spiritual masters. We will never know. He was electrocuted by an electric fan after a shower and died.

One might say, however, that in his ending was his beginning. Certainly, his life–his quest–has inspired many people. "A sinless life is like pure art," Auden wrote, in a 1944 letter to Clement Greenburg. "You must strive for it at the same time that you know it is impossible, and if you forget the impossibility, the life, like the poetry, ceases to be."

SELECTED BIBLIOGRAPHY

William Blake, "All Religions Are One," in *The Norton Anthology of English Literature* (New York: Norton, 1986).

Albert Camus, *Notebooks 1935-1942* (New York: Random House, 1965).

Albert Einstein, "The Pacifist Problem," *Ideas and Opinions* (New York: The Modern Library, 1996).

Sharon Ghamari-Tabrizi, *The Worlds of Herman Kahn* (Cambridge: Harvard University Press, 2005).

John Howard Griffin, *Follow the Ecstasy: Thomas Merton, The Hermitage Years 1965-1968* (Ft. Worth TX, Latitudes Press, 1983).

Sam Hamill and J. P. Seaton, ed. and trans., *The Poetry of Zen* (Boston: Shambhala, 2004).

Glen Hinson, "A Mertonesque Catholic Image," talk delivered at Bellarmine University, August 16, 2005.

Bert Hornback, *Talking About Poetry* (Louisville: Bellarmine University Press, 2002)

Jack Kerouac, *The Dharma Bums* (New York: Penguin, 1958).

Arthur Kirsch, *Auden and Christianity* (New Haven: Yale University Press, 2005).

Denise Levertov, *Live Coals* (New York: New Directions, 1964).

Thomas Merton, *The Collected Poems of Thomas Merton* (New York: New Directions, 1977).

_____, *The Geography of Lograire* (New York: New Directions, 1969).

_____, *The Intimate Merton: His Life from Journals*, ed. Patrick Hart and Jonathan Montaldo, (San Francisco: HarperCollins, 1999).

_____, *New Seeds of Contemplation* (New York: New Directions, 1972).

_____, ed., *Monks Pond* (Lexington, KY: The University Press of Kentucky, 1989).

_____, *Passion for Peace: The Social Essays*, ed. William H. Shannon, (New York: Crossroad, 1995).

_____, *The Seven Storey Mountain* (New York: Harcourt Brace & Co., 1948).

_____, *The Way of Chuang Tzu* (New York: New Directions, 1965).

_____, *Witness to Freedom: Letters in Times of Crisis*, ed. William H. Shannon (New York: Farrar Straus & Giroux, 1994).

_____, and Jonathan Greene, *On the Banks of Monks Pond, The Thomas Merton/Jonathan Greene Correspondence* (Frankfort: Broadstone Books Kentucky, 2004).

_____, and Czeslaw Milosz, *Striving Towards Being: The Letters of Thomas Merton and Czeslaw Milosz*, ed. Robert Faggen (New York: Farrar, Straus & Giroux, 1997).

Charles Simic, *The Unemployed Fortune-Teller* (Ann Arbor: The University of Michigan Press, 1994).

John Jeremiah Sullivan, "Faith and Doubt in Kentucky," *Oxford American* (No. 33, 2004).

Lynn Szabo, "'Hiding the Ace of Freedoms': Discovering the Way(s) of Peace in Thomas Merton's *Cables to the Ace*," in *The Merton Annual* 15 (2002).

Bonnie Thurston, "Islam in Alaska: Sufi Material in *Thomas Merton in Alaska*," in *The Merton Seasonal* (Vol. 29, No. 4).

_____, "Some Reflections on Islamic Poems by Thomas Merton," in *The World in My Bloodstream: Thomas Merton's Universal Embrace,* ed. Angus Stuart (Wales, UK: Three Peaks Press, 2004).

Virginia Woolf, *Three Guineas* (New York: Harcourt Brace & Co., 1966).

ABOUT THE AUTHOR

Frederick Smock is the poet-in-residence at Bellarmine University, in Louisville, where he received the 2005 Wyatt Faculty Award. He has published seven books, three of them poetry with Larkspur Press, most recently *Guest House*. His book of essays, *Poetry & Compassion: Essays on Art & Craft*, was published in the fall of 2006. He is the recipient of the Henry Leadingham Poetry Prize, the Jim Wayne Miller Prize for Poetry, and an Al Smith Fellowship in Poetry from the Kentucky Arts Council. His poems have appeared in *Poetry, The Iowa Review, The Southern Review,* and others. Mr. Smock lives in Louisville with his wife, the writer and actress Olga-Maria Cruz.

This book has been designed & typeset
by Jonathan Greene using Monotype Dante
for the text and Monotype Bell for display.
Printing and binding by Thomson-Shore.